The Wisdom of

HESCHEL

BOOKS BY ABRAHAM JOSHUA HESCHEL

Abraham Joshua Heschel

The Wisdom of

HESCHEL

Selected by Ruth Marcus Goodhill

FARRAR, STRAUS AND GIROUX

NEW YORK

First printing, 1975
Printed in the United States of America
Published simultaneously in Canada by
McGraw-Hill Ryerson Ltd., Toronto
Designed by Guy Fleming

Library of Congress Cataloging in Publication Data
Heschel, Abraham Joshua, 1907–1972.
The wisdom of Heschel.
Bibliography: p.
1. Judaism—Quotations, maxims, etc.   2. Re-
ligion—Quotations, maxims, etc.   I. Title.
BM45.H455   1975   296'.08   75-15945

To Dean and Barbara

Contents

ABRAHAM JOSHUA HESCHEL, one of the great
creative Jewish scholars and thinkers, was born in
Warsaw in 1907. A descendant of a long line of
scholars going back to the sixteenth century, his
intensive early education in Torah and Talmud was
imbued with piety. He entered the University of
Berlin in 1927 and received his Ph.D. in philosophy
in 1933. While a student at the university, he also
studied at the Hochschule für die Wissenschaft
des Judentums (Academy for Jewish Studies).
In 1936, "Die Prophetie," his dissertation, was
published. It later became part of his classic work
The Prophets, published in English in 1962.

In 1937, Martin Buber chose Heschel as his
successor at the Judisches Lehrhaus of Frankfurt
am Main. But the clouds of anti-Semitism darkened
and Jews of Polish citizenship were expelled from
Germany in 1938. After a brief return to Warsaw
in 1939, he left for London—only two months
before the German invasion of Poland and the
holocaust that followed. Heschel narrowly escaped
extermination at the hands of the Nazis. He
described himself as "a brand plucked from the fire,
in which my people was burned to death . . .
millions of human lives were exterminated to evil's
greater glory . . ."

In 1940 he came to the United States to join the faculty of Hebrew Union College in Cincinnati, where he remained for five years as Professor of Philosophy and Rabbinics. From 1945 until his death, he was Professor of Jewish Ethics and Mysticism at the Jewish Theological Seminary of America. In 1965–6, he was the first Harry Emerson Fosdick Visiting Lecturer at Union Theological Seminary. He also lectured at the universities of Minnesota, Iowa, and Stanford.

Rabbi Heschel was a devout Jew whose compassion embraced all mankind. "My major concern is the human situation," he once said. "I maintain that the agony of contemporary man is the agony of the spiritually stunted man." In the same spirit he held that "the main theme of Jewish law is the person rather than an institution," and that "the highest peak of spiritual living is not necessarily reached in rare moments of ecstasy; the highest peak lies wherever we are and may be ascended in a common deed. Religion is not made for extraordinary occasions." He epitomized his interpretation of law in this definition: "An act of injustice is condemned, not because the law is broken, but because a person has been hurt."

Heschel was in the forefront of every human

concern. In the spring of 1965, he marched with
Martin Luther King, Jr., at Selma, Alabama; he
was a leader in the protests against American policy
in Vietnam; he participated in many civil-rights
marches and peace rallies. Following the Six-Day
War in 1967, he responded to the historic moment
with his book *Israel: An Echo of Eternity*. He was
one of the first to urge world Jewry to come to
the aid of Soviet Jews. He was a strong ecumenicist,
urging Christian-Jewish dialogue. He was frequently
invited to the Vatican and was asked to speak on
prayer on Italian radio and television. Although
he suffered a near-fatal heart attack in 1969, he
continued his strenuous activities in behalf of
human rights.

All humanity was his concern. "To be human,"
he said, "is to be involved, to act and to react, to
wonder and to respond. For man to be is to play a
part in a cosmic drama, knowingly or unknowingly."
As he saw it, "Living involves responsible understanding of one's role in relation to all other beings."
He also wrote: "God in the universe is a spirit of
concern for life . . . We often fail in trying to
understand Him, not because we do not know how
to extend our concepts far enough, but because we
do not know how to begin close enough. To think

of God is not to find Him as an object in our minds, but to find ourselves in Him."

Following his sudden death, tribute was paid to him the world over. In this country, the Jesuit publication *America* devoted an entire issue (March 10, 1973) to Heschel's memory. The editor stated: "Each of you, our readers, will have his own lesson to learn from Abraham Joshua Heschel as he speaks to you of the living tradition of Judaism, in all its energy, holiness and compassion. May the God whom Jews, Christians and Muslims worship bring us to live together in peace and understanding and mutual appreciation."

Rev. Dr. John C. Bennett wrote in the same issue: "Abraham Heschel belonged to the whole American religious community. I know of no other person of whom this was so true . . ." Dr. Bennett was president of Union Theological Seminary when Dr. Heschel served as a Visiting Professor.

Professor Fritz A. Rothschild of the Jewish Theological Seminary wrote in *America:* "We find ourselves confronted with a style that exhibits a beauty and vividness of phrase rarely found in scholarly works. The ideas appear in aphoristic flashes of insight . . . spiritual gems . . . the easy-flowing prose hides subtle and complex thought processes that are ours to discover only if we delve beneath the smooth surface and study each passage in depth."

My selections from the works of Abraham Joshua Heschel represent a personal response to his prophetic genius. This book, conceived during his lifetime, is offered as an introduction to his thought and to his profound insight into the agonies of modern society. As such, this anthology focuses on one idea, sometimes one phrase, at a time; it attempts, in his own words, "to stand still and consider."

The idea for this book was born in 1971. When Professor Heschel and his wife, Sylvia, visited our home in December of that year, I showed him my preliminary outline, which he studied carefully. During the following year he offered practical implementation for its publication. He introduced me to Lily Edelman, B'nai B'rith's director of adult education, who subsequently played a major role in seeing the book through to fulfillment.

Choosing selections from Heschel's many works was an awesome responsibility. I received great encouragement throughout from Sylvia Heschel, whose enthusiasm, cooperation, and friendship remain a source of inspiration. My concern for and involvement in Judaism were deeply influenced by the Brandeis Camp Institute experiences over many years (Dr. Shlomo Bardin, Founder-Director). My appreciation is due to Susannah Heschel, who follows in her father's footsteps, preparing to teach theology and philosophy; to Dr. George Shecter for his constant interest; and to Christine Davis for secretarial assistance.

I approached the task with reticence. Thanks to the unfailing encouragement of my husband, Dr. Victor Goodhill, I was inspired to complete this labor of love.

We were expecting the Heschels for a visit with us here on December 24, 1972. On December 23, Shabbat Vayechi 5733, Rabbi Abraham Joshua Heschel died in his sleep.

RUTH MARCUS GOODHILL

Los Angeles
March 24, 1975

PHILOSOPHY may be defined as the art of asking the right questions . . . Awareness of the problems outlives all solutions. The answers are questions in disguise, every new answer giving rise to new questions.

HESCHEL, *God in Search of Man*

Questions Man
Asks

———————

WHAT IS THE meaning of my being?
. . . My quest—man's quest—is not for
theoretical knowledge about myself . . .
What I look for is not how to gain a firm
hold on myself and on life, but primarily
how to live a life that would deserve and
evoke an eternal Amen.

It is not enough for me to be able
to say "I am"; I want to know *who I am,*
and in relation to whom I live. It is not
enough for me to ask questions; I want to
know how to answer the one question that
seems to encompass everything I face:
What am I here for?

IT IS NOT ONLY the question of how to justify our own existence but, above all, how to justify bringing human beings into the world. If human existence is absurd and miserable, why give birth to children?

Do we build cities in order to supply
ruins for the archaeologists of a later age?
Do we rear children in order to prepare
ashes for the outcome of nuclear wars?

THE IMPERATIVE according to the logic of biology may be: "Eat, drink, and be merry!" Yet a life essentially dedicated to the fulfillment of such an imperative results in depriving human being of all the qualities of being human.

WHY BE CONCERNED with meaning? Why not be content with satisfaction of desires and needs? The vital drives of food, sex, and power, as well as the mental functions aimed at satisfying them, are as characteristic of animals as they are of man. Being human is a characteristic of a being who faces the question: *After satisfaction, what?*

MAN CANNOT RESTRAIN his bitter yearning to know whether life is nothing but a series of momentary physiological and mental processes, actions, and forms of behavior, a flow of vicissitudes, desires, and sensations, running like grains through an hourglass, marking time only once and always vanishing . . . Is life nothing but an agglomeration of facts, unrelated to one another—chaos camouflaged by illusion?

MAN CANNOT be understood in his own terms. He can only be understood in terms of a larger context. Our problem, now, is: What is the context of man, in terms of which he can be ultimately understood?

To BE HUMAN is to be involved, to act and to react, to wonder and to respond. For man, to be is to play a part in a cosmic drama, knowingly or unknowingly . . . Man's most important problem is not being but living. To live means to be at the crossroads. There are many forces and drives within the self. What direction to take is a question we face again and again. Who am I? A mere chip from the block of being? Am I not both the chisel and the marble? Being and foreseeing? Being and bringing into being?

Who Is Man?

ALL THAT EXISTS obeys. Man alone occupies a unique status. As a natural being he obeys, as a human being he must frequently choose; confined in his existence, he is unrestrained in his will. His acts do not emanate from him like rays of energy from matter. Placed in the parting of the ways, he must time and again decide which direction to take. The course of his life is, accordingly, unpredictable; no one can write his autobiography in advance.

MAN IS A FOUNTAIN of immense
meaning, not only a drop in the ocean of
being. The human species is too powerful,
too dangerous, to be a mere toy or a freak
of the Creator. He undoubtedly represents
something unique in the great body of the
universe.

THE EXPANSION of human power has hardly begun, and what man is going to do with his power may either save or destroy our planet. The earth may be of small significance within the infinite universe. But if it is of some significance, man holds the key to it.

THERE IS ALWAYS more than one path
to go, and we are forced to be free—we are
free against our will—and have the audacity
to choose, rarely knowing how or why.

WE ARE IN the minority in the great realm of being, and with a genius for adjustment, we frequently seek to join the multitude. We are in the minority within our own nature, and in the agony and battle of passions we often choose to envy the beast. We behave as if the animal kingdom were our lost paradise, to which we are trying to return for moments of delight, believing that it is the animal state in which happiness consists.

MAN IS MORE than what he is to
himself. In his reason he may be limited,
in his will he may be wicked, yet he stands
in a relation to God which he may betray
but not sever, and which constitutes the
essential meaning of his life. He is the knot
in which heaven and earth are interlaced.

How Shall Man Live?

How SHOULD MAN, a being created
in the likeness of God, live? What way of
living is compatible with the grandeur and
mystery of living?

IT IS in *deeds* that man becomes aware of what his life really is, of his power to harm and to hurt, to wreck and to ruin; of his ability to derive joy and to bestow it on others; to relieve and to increase his own and other people's tensions . . . What he may not dare to think, he often utters in deeds. The heart is revealed in the deeds.

THE DEED is the test, the trial, and the risk. What we perform may seem slight, but the aftermath is immense. An individual's misdeed can be the beginning of a nation's disaster.

IF MAN were able to survey at a glance all
he has done in the course of his life, what
would he feel? He would be terrified at the
extent of his own power . . . A single deed
may place the lives of countless men in
the chains of its unpredictable effects.

NOT THINGS but deeds are the source of our sad perplexities. Confronted with a world of things, man unloosens a tide of deeds. The fabulous fact of man's ability to act, *the wonder of doing,* is no less amazing than the marvel of being.

WE STAND on a razor's edge. It is so

easy to hurt, to destroy, to insult, to kill.

Giving birth to one child is a mystery;

bringing death to millions is but a skill. It

is not quite within the power of the human

will to generate life; it is quite within the

power of the will to destroy life.

JUDAISM TAKES DEEDS more seriously
than things. Jewish law is, in a sense, *a
science of deeds* . . . Every deed is a
problem; there is a unique task at every
moment. All of life at all moments is the
problem and the task.

Man's Needs

THE PROBLEM of living does not arise with the question of how to take care of the rascals or with the realization of how we blunder in dealing with other people. It begins in the relation to our own selves, in the handling of our physiological and emotional functions. What is first at stake in the life of man is not the fact of sin, of the wrong and corrupt, but the natural acts, the *needs*. Our possessions pose no less a problem than our passions.

EVERY HUMAN BEING is a cluster of needs, some of which are indigenous to his nature, while others are induced by advertisement, fashion, envy, or come about as miscarriages of authentic needs.

WE USUALLY FAIL to discern between authentic and artificial needs and, misjudging a whim for an aspiration, we are thrown into ugly tensions. Most obsessions are the perpetuation of such misjudgments. In fact, more people die in the epidemics of needs than in the epidemics of disease.

THERE ARE no material wants that science and technology do not promise to supply. To stem the expansion of man's needs, which in turn is brought about by technological and social advancement, would mean to halt the stream on which civilization is riding. Yet the stream unchecked may sweep away civilization itself, since the pressure of needs turned into aggressive interests is the constant cause of wars and increases in direct proportion to technological progress.

NEEDS ARE LOOKED UPON today as if they were holy, as if they contained the quintessence of eternity. Needs are our gods, and we toil and spare no effort to gratify them. Suppression of a desire is considered a sacrilege that must inevitably avenge itself in the form of some mental disorder.

SHORT IS THE WAY from need to greed. Evil conditions make us seethe with evil needs, with mad dreams. Can we afford to pursue all our innate needs, even our will for power?

HE WHO SETS OUT to employ the realities of life as means for satisfying his own desires will soon forfeit his freedom and be degraded to a mere tool. Acquiring things, he becomes enslaved to them; in subduing others, he loses his own soul.

WE FEEL JAILED in the confinement of personal needs. The more we indulge in satisfactions, the deeper is our feeling of oppressiveness. To be an iconoclast of idolized needs, to defy our own immoral interests, though they seem to be vital and have long been cherished, we must be able to say *no* to ourselves in the name of a higher *yes*.

Is Man Needed?

ANIMALS ARE CONTENT when their
needs are satisfied; man insists not only on
being satisfied but also on being able to
satisfy, on *being a need* . . . Personal needs
come and go, but one anxiety remains:
Am I needed? There is no man who has
not been moved by that anxiety.

SOPHISTICATED THINKING may enable man to feign his being sufficient to himself. Yet the way to insanity is paved with such illusions. The feeling of futility that comes with the sense of being useless, of not being needed in the world, is the most common cause of psychoneurosis.

THE ONLY WAY to avoid despair is *to be a need* rather than an end. *Happiness,* in fact, may be defined as the *certainty of being needed.* But *who* is in need of man?

DOES MAN EXIST for the sake of society?
. . . The ultimate worth of a person would
then be determined by his usefulness to
others, by the efficiency of his social work
. . . Such service does not claim all of one's
life and can therefore not be the ultimate
answer to his quest for the meaning of
life as a whole. Man has more to give than
what other men are able or willing to accept.

MAN'S QUEST for a meaning of existence is essentially a quest for the lasting . . . The way to the lasting does not lie on the other side of life; it does not begin where time breaks off. The lasting begins not beyond but *within time*, within the moment, within the concrete . . . The days of our lives are representatives of eternity rather than fugitives, and we must live as if the fate of all of time would totally depend on a single moment.

MAN *is* meaning . . . All our experiences are needs, dissolving when the needs
are fulfilled. But the truth is, our existence,
too, is a need . . . There is a need for
our lives, and in living we satisfy it . . .
Our needs are temporal, while our being
needed is lasting.

MAN IS NOT an innocent bystander in the cosmic drama. There is in us more kinship with the divine than we are able to believe. The souls of men are candles of the Lord, lit on the cosmic way, rather than fireworks produced by the combustion of nature's explosive compositions, and every soul is indispensable to Him. Man is needed, he is *a need of God.*

Man's Ultimate

Purpose

———

HUMAN LIFE consists of needs as a house consists of bricks, yet an accumulation of needs is no more a life than a heap of bricks is a house. Life as a whole is related to a purpose, to an end . . . It is the distinction of man to be concerned with ends, not only with needs.

To HAVE a goal before one's eyes, to pursue it and to keep on extending it, seems to be the way of civilized living. It is typical of the debauchee to adjust his ends to his selfish needs. He is always ready to conform to his needs. Indeed, anybody can be taught to have needs and to indulge in costly food, dress, or anything which satisfies the appetites or tastes.

FREE MEN are not blind in obeying
needs but, weighing and comparing their
relative merits, they will seek to satisfy those
which contribute to the enhancement and
enrichment of higher values. In other words,
they would approve only of those needs
that serve the attainment of good ends . . .
Psychological fatalism, which maintains
that there is only one way, an animal way,
is a paralyzing fallacy to which the spirit
of man will never surrender.

CIVILIZED LIVING is the result of that
urge, of that drive to proceed in our efforts
beyond immediate needs, beyond individual,
tribal, or national goals.

THE URGE to build a family, to serve society, or to dedicate oneself to art and science, may often originate in the desire to satisfy one's own appetite or ambition. Yet, seen from the watchtower of history, the selfish usefulness of required deeds, the possibility of regarding them as instrumental to the attainment of one's own selfish goals, is God's secret weapon in his struggle with man's callousness.

FOR WHOM does he plant who plants a tree? For generations to come, for faces he has never seen. Higher purposes are shrewdly disguised as ends of immediate usefulness. It is as if a *divine cunning* operated in human history, using our instincts as pretexts for the attainment of goals which are universally valid, a scheme to harness man's lower forces in the service of higher ends.

MAN'S UNDERSTANDING of *what* is right
and wrong has often varied throughout
the ages; yet the consciousness *that* there is
a distinction between right and wrong
is permanent and universal.

What Are the Problems?

MAN IS A PROBLEM intrinsically and
under all circumstances. To be human is to
be a problem, and the problem expresses
itself in anguish, in the mental suffering of
man. Every human being has at least a
vague notion, image, or dream of what
humanity ought to be, of how human nature
ought to act. The problem of man is
occasioned by our coming upon a conflict
or contradiction between existence and
expectation, between what man is and what
is expected of him.

MAN IS ENDOWED with an amazing degree of receptivity, conformity, and gullibility. He is never finished, never immutable. Humanity is not something he comes upon in the recesses of the self. He always looks for a model or an example to follow. What determines one's being human is the image one adopts.

NEW IN THIS AGE is an unparalleled *Existentialism etc.*
awareness of the terrifying seriousness of the
human situation. Questions we seriously
ask today would have seemed utterly absurd
twenty years ago, such as, for example: Are
we the last generation? Is this the very
last hour for Western civilization?

PHILOSOPHY cannot be the same after Auschwitz and Hiroshima. Certain assumptions about humanity have proved to be specious, have been smashed. What has long been regarded as commonplace has proved to be utopianism.

Phil = moral/ethics.

Agree !

PHILOSOPHY, to be relevant, must offer us a wisdom to live by—relevant not only in the isolation of our study rooms but also in moments of facing staggering cruelty and the threat of disaster. The question of man must be pondered not only in the halls of learning but also in the presence of inmates in extermination camps, and in the sight of the mushroom of a nuclear explosion.

WHAT IS HAPPENING in the life of
man, and how are we to grasp it? We ask
in order to know how to live.

ONE CANNOT STUDY the condition of
man without being touched by the plight
of man. Though biologically intact, man
is essentially afflicted with a sense of
helplessness, discontent, inferiority, fear.
Outwardly Homo sapiens may pretend to
be satisfied and strong; inwardly he is
poor, needy, vulnerable, always on the
verge of misery, prone to suffer mentally and
physically. Scratch his skin and you come
upon bereavement, affliction, uncertainty,
fear, and pain.

DISPARITY between man's appearance and reality is a condition of social integration. Suppressions are the price he pays for being accepted in society. Adjustment involves assenting to odd auspices, concessions of conscience, inevitable hypocrisies. It is, indeed, often a life of "quiet desperation."

Rousseau

WHAT IS BEING HUMAN? . . . Man's physical and mental reality is beyond dispute; his meaning, his spiritual relevance, is a question that cries for an answer. Is it not right to suggest that the agony of the contemporary man is the agony of a spiritually stunted man?

Man's PLIGHT is not due to the fear of
non-being, to the fear of death, but to the
fear of living, because all living is branded
with unerasable shock at absurdity, cruelty,
and callousness experienced in the past.
A human being is a being in fear of pain,
in fear of being put to shame.

THE FEAR OF LIVING arises most
commonly out of experiences of failure or
insult, of having gone astray or having been
rebuffed. It is rooted in the encounter with
other human beings, in not knowing how
to be with other beings, in the inability
or refusal to communicate, but above all in
the failure to live in complete involvement
with what transcends our living.

What Is Troubling the Family?

———

HOME, inwardness, friendship, conversation are becoming obsolete. Instead of
insisting: my home is my castle, we
confess: my car is my home. We have
no friends; we have business associates.
Conversation is disappearing; watching
television substitutes for the expression of
ideas.

THE MODERN MAN has not only forgotten how to be alone; he finds it difficult even to be with his fellow man. He not only runs away from himself; he runs away from his family.

THE HEART of the Ten Commandments is to be found in the words: *Revere thy father and thy mother*. Without profound reverence for father and mother, our ability to observe the other commandments is dangerously impaired.

REVERENCE FOR PARENTS is the fundamental form of reverence, for in the parent is incarnated the mystery of man's coming into being. Rejection of the parent is a repudiation of the mystery. Only a person who lives in a way which is compatible with the mystery of human existence is capable of evoking reverence in the child. The basic problem is the parent, not the child.

THE PROBLEM is why my child should revere me. Unless my child will sense in my personal existence acts and attitudes that evoke reverence—the ability to delay satisfactions, to overcome prejudices, to sense the holy, to strive for the noble— why should he/she revere me?

WE ARE CONCERNED for what is happening all over the country: so many broken
homes, disintegrated families, alienated
boys, runaway girls, parents in despair,
teachers in disgust. It is a serious malaise,
and let us not deceive ourselves . . . At a
time when the institution of the family is
in distress and under attack, it is important
to be reminded that the home remains the
finest model of human living and the
family—the finest form of fellowship.

THE CRISIS of the family is a crisis of the home. Home is where we love, where we dream, where we live with authenticity, where the core is revealed. Home is where we learn what values to cherish, what goals to be committed to, as well as the meaning of being committed.

THE CENTER of Judaism is <u>in the home</u>. In contrast to other religions, it is at home where the essential celebrations and acts of observance take place—rather than in the synagogue or temple . . . The synagogue is an auxiliary . . . A Jewish home is where Judaism is at home, where Jewish learning, commitment, sensitivity to values are cultivated and cherished.

WHAT IS CHARACTERISTIC of the modern family is that on the level of profound personal experience, parents and children live apart. The experiences shared at home are perfunctory rather than creative. In the past, it was the role of the father to lead the children through moments of exaltation . . . Now we are entering a social structure in which the father is becoming obsolete . . . The husband of the mother is not a father; he is a regular guy, a playmate for the boys, engaged in the same foibles and subject to similar impulses.

Teaching Our
Young

THE PROBLEM of our youth is not youth. The problem is the spirit of our age: denial of transcendence, the vapidity of values, emptiness in the heart, the decreased sensitivity to the imponderable quality of the spirit, the collapse of communication between the realm of tradition and the inner world of the individual. The central problem is that we do not know how to think, how to pray, how to cry, how to resist the deceptions of too many persuaders.

THE PROBLEM will not be solved by implanting in youth a sense of belonging. Belonging to a society that fails in offering opportunities to satisfy authentic human needs will not soothe the sense of frustration and rebellion. What youth needs is a sense of significant being, a sense of reverence for the society to which we all belong.

WE, the adults, have delegated our moral responsibility to the schools, the social agencies, or the community funds . . . Significantly, the Biblical injunction does not say that we are to appoint a teacher to train our children. The Biblical injunction is that the parent be the teacher . . . The teacher is but a representative of the father, according to Jewish tradition. Thou shalt teach them diligently, not vicariously.

Our society is fostering the *segregation of youth*, the separation of young and old. The adult has no fellowship with the young. He has little to say to the young, and there is little opportunity for the young to share the wisdom of experience, or the experience of maturity.

WE HAVE DENIED our young people the knowledge of the dark side of life. They see a picture of ease, play, and fun. That life includes hardships, illness, grief, even agony; that many hearts are sick with bitterness, resentfulness, envy—are facts of which young people have hardly an awareness. They do not feel morally challenged, they do not feel called upon.

THE YOUNG PERSON of today is pampered. In moments of crisis he transfers his guilt to others. Society, the age, or his mother is blamed for his failure. Weakened by self-indulgence, he breaks down easily under hardship.

DEMANDS which were made of the individual in earlier periods are now considered excessive. Self-discipline is obsolescent, self-denial unhygienic, metaphysical problems irrelevant. The terms of reference are emotional release and suppression, with little regard for remorse and responsibility . . . Self-respect is the fruit of discipline; the sense of dignity grows with the ability to say no to oneself.

WE PREPARE the pupil for employment, for holding a job. We do not teach him how to be a person, how to resist conformity, how to grow inwardly, how to say no to his own self. We teach him how to adjust to the public; we do not teach him how to cultivate privacy.

We TELL THE PUPIL many things, but
what has our instruction to do with his
inner problems, with the way he is going
to behave or think outside the classroom?
In our classroom we shy away from fundamental issues. How should one deal with
evil? What shall one do about envy? What
is the meaning of honesty? How should
one face the problem of loneliness? What
has religion to say about war and violence?
About indifference and evil?

Do we prepare the student for years of going through tensions, of facing ordeals and tribulations? Man is born to face temptations and to make decisions. He is born to insist as well as to resist. There is neither faith nor integrity without awareness of the difficulty of faith and the arduousness of integrity. The task is to develop convictions as well as spiritual audacity.

FOR LACK OF moral and spiritual sources of exaltation, our young people turn to drugs . . . In order to experience a moment of exaltation, young people are ready to destroy their lives, to sacrifice an authenticity of soul which they never acquired in our soulless system of education.

Caring for Our
Old

I SEE THE SICK and the despised, the defeated and the bitter, the rejected and the lonely. I see them clustered together and alone, clinging to a hope for somebody's affection that does not come to pass. I hear them pray for the release that comes with death. I see them deprived and forgotten, masters yesterday, outcasts today.

WHAT WE OWE the old is reverence,

but all they ask for is consideration,

attention, not to be discarded and forgotten.

What they deserve is preference, yet we do

not even grant them equality. One father

finds it possible to sustain a dozen children,

yet a dozen children find it impossible to

sustain one father.

CARE FOR THE OLD is regarded as an act of charity rather than as a supreme privilege. In the never-dying utterance of the Ten Commandments, the God of Israel did not proclaim: Honor me, revere me. He proclaimed instead: Revere your father and your mother. There is no reverence for God without reverence for father and mother.

MORE MONEY and time are spent on
the art of concealing the signs of old age
than on the art of dealing with heart disease
or cancer . . . Being old is a defeat, something to be ashamed of. Authenticity and
honesty of existence are readily exchanged
for false luster, for camouflage, sham, and
deception. A gray hair may destroy the
chance for promotion, may cost a salesman
his job, and may inwardly alienate a son
from his father.

A VAST AMOUNT of human misery, as well as enormous cultural and spiritual damage, is due to these twin phenomena of our civilization: contempt for the old and the traumatic fear of getting old. Monotheism has acquired a new meaning: the one and only thing that counts is being young. Youth is our god, and being young is divine. To be sure, youth is a very marvelous thing. However, the cult of youth is idolatry. Abraham is the grand old man, but the legend of Faust is pagan.

THE TEST of a people is how it behaves
toward the old. It is easy to love children.
Even tyrants and dictators make a point
of being fond of children. But affection and
care for the old, the incurable, the helpless,
are the true gold mines of a culture.

WHILE WE DO NOT officially define old age as a second childhood, some of the programs we devise are highly effective in helping the aged to become children. The popular approach is: "Keep alive a zest for living in the elderly by encouraging them to continue old hobbies or to develop new ones." The effect is a pickled existence, preserved in brine with spices.

Is this the way and goal of existence: to study, grow, toil, mature, and reach the age of retirement in order to live like a child? After all, *to be retired does not mean to be retarded.*

WHAT IS the role of recreation in the life of the aged? . . . An overindulgence in recreational activities aggravates rather than ameliorates the condition it is trying to deal with, namely *the trivialization of existence*. In the past it was ritual and prayer that staved off that danger.

WHAT ARE the basic spiritual ills of old

age? The sense of being useless to, and

rejected by, family and society; the sense

of inner emptiness and boredom; loneliness

and the fear of time.

MAY I SUGGEST that man's potential for change and growth is much greater than we are willing to admit and that old age be regarded not as the age of stagnation but as *the age of opportunities for inner growth?* The old person must not be treated as a patient, or regard his retirement as a prolonged state of resignation.

ONE OUGHT TO ENTER old age the way
one enters the senior year at a university, in
exciting anticipation of consummation.
Rich in perspective, experienced in failure,
the person advanced in years is capable of
shedding prejudices and the fever of
vested interests. He does not see any more
in every fellow man a person who stands in
his way, and competitiveness may cease to
be his way of thinking.

PEOPLE ARE ANXIOUS to save up
financial means for old age; they should
also be anxious to prepare a spiritual income
for old age . . . Wisdom, maturity,
tranquillity do not come all of a sudden
when we retire from business. We must
begin teaching in public schools about the
wisdom and peace that arrive in old age.
Reverence for the old must be an essential
part of elementary education at school,
and particularly at home. *Education for
retirement* is a life-long process.

REVERENCE FOR THE OLD, dialogue between generations, is as important to the dignity of the young as it is for the well-being of the old. We deprive ourselves by disparaging the old.

Relating to the
World

THERE ARE three ways in which we may
relate ourselves to the world—we may
exploit it, we may enjoy it, we may accept
it in awe.

OUR AGE is one in which usefulness is
thought to be the chief merit of nature;
in which the attainment of power, the
utilization of its resources, is taken to be
the chief purpose of man in God's creation.
Man has indeed become primarily a
tool-making animal, and the world is now a
gigantic tool box for the satisfaction of his
needs.

THE GREEKS learned in order to comprehend. The Hebrews learned in order to revere. The modern man learns in order to use . . . Knowledge means success. We do not know any more how to justify any value except in terms of expediency.

WE TEACH children how to measure, how to weigh. We fail to teach them how to revere, how to sense wonder and awe. The sense of the sublime, the sign of the inward greatness of the human soul and something which is potentially given to all men, is now a rare gift.

THE SUBLIME may be sensed in things
of beauty as well as in acts of goodness and
in the search for truth . . . The sublime
is not necessarily related to the vast and
the overwhelming in size. It may be sensed
in every grain of sand, in every drop of
water. Every flower in the summer, every
snowflake in the winter, may arouse in us
the sense of wonder that is our response to
the sublime.

MAN SEES the things that surround him long before he becomes aware of his own self. Many of us are conscious of the hiddenness of things, but few of us sense the mystery of our own presence. The self cannot be described in the terms of the mind, for all our symbols are too poor to render it.

Wonder...Radical

Amazement...

Awe

―――

WONDER or radical amazement is a
prerequisite for an authentic awareness of
that which is; it refers not only to what we
see but also to the very act of seeing, as
well as to our own selves, to the selves that
see and are amazed at their ability to see.

GRANDEUR or mystery is something with which we are confronted everywhere and at all times. Even the very act of thinking baffles our thinking, just as every intelligible fact is, by virtue of its being a fact, drunk with baffling aloofness. Does not mystery reign within reasoning, within perception, within explanation?

WHERE IS the self-understanding that
could unfurl the marvel of our own thinking,
that could explain the grace of our emptying
the concrete with charms of abstraction?
What formula could explain and solve the
enigma of the very fact of thinking? . . .
The most incomprehensible fact is the fact
that we comprehend at all.

As CIVILIZATION advances, the sense of wonder declines. Such decline is an alarming symptom of our state of mind. Mankind will not perish for want of information; but only for want of appreciation.

IN RADICAL AMAZEMENT, the Biblical
man faces *"the great things and unsearch-
able, the wondrous things without number"*
(Job 5:9) . . . Not only do the things
outside him evoke the amazement of the
Biblical man; his own being fills him with
awe.

I will give thanks unto Thee,

For I am fearfully and marvelously made;

Wondrous are thy works;

And that my soul knoweth exceedingly.

(Psalms 139:14)

"REPLETE IS THE WORLD with a spiritual radiance, replete with sublime and marvelous secrets. But a small hand held against the eye hides it all," said the Baal Shem* . . . We fail to wonder . . . This is the tragedy of every man: "to dim all wonder by indifference." Life is routine, and routine is resistance to the wonder.

* Founder of Hasidism.

AWE IS an act of insight into a meaning greater than ourselves . . . *The beginning of awe is wonder, and the beginning of wisdom is awe* . . . Awe is a way of being in rapport with the mystery of all reality.

THE MEANING OF AWE is to realize
that life takes place under wide horizons,
horizons that range beyond the span of an
individual life or even the life of a nation,
a generation, or an era.

AWE ENABLES US to perceive in the world intimations of the divine, to sense in small things the beginning of infinite significance, to sense the ultimate in the common and the simple; to feel in the rush of the passing the stillness of the eternal.

Awe precedes faith; it is *at the root of faith.* We must grow in awe in order to reach faith. Awe rather than faith is the cardinal attitude of the religious Jew.

THERE IS only one way to wisdom:
awe. Forfeit your sense of awe, let your
conceit diminish your ability to revere, and
the universe becomes a marketplace for
you. The loss of awe is the great block to
insight . . . The greatest insights happen
to us in moments of awe.

A RETURN to reverence is the first prerequisite for a revival of wisdom.

How DO WE SEEK to apprehend the
world? . . . When trying to hold an
interview with reality face to face, without
the aid of either words or concepts, we
realize that what is intelligible to our mind
is but a thin surface of the profoundly
undisclosed, a ripple of inveterate silence
that remains immune to curiosity and
inquisitiveness like distant foliage in the
dusk.

WHAT SMITES US with unquenchable
amazement is not that which we grasp
and are able to convey but that which
lies within our reach but beyond our
grasp; not the quantitative aspect of
nature but something qualitative . . . the
true meaning, source, and end of being;
in other words, the ineffable.

THE INEFFABLE inhabits the magnificent
[com]mon, the grandiose and the
of reality alike. Some people
s quality at distant intervals in
extrac.inary events; others sense it in the
ordinary events, in every fold, in every nook;
day after day, hour after hour. To them
things are bereft of triteness . . . Slight
and simple as things may be—a piece of
paper, a morsel of bread, a word, a sigh—
they hide a never-ending secret: a glimpse
of God? kinship with the spirit of being?
an eternal flash of a will?

ANALYZE, weigh, and measure a tree
as you please, observe and describe its form
and functions, its genesis and the laws to
which it is subject; still an *acquaintance*
with its *essence* never comes about . . .
The awareness of the unknown is earlier
than the awareness of the known. The tree
of knowledge grows upon the soil of
mystery.

SCIENCE DOES NOT TRY to fathom the mystery. It merely describes and explains the way in which things behave in terms of causal necessity . . . Science extends rather than limits the scope of the ineffable, and our radical amazement is enhanced rather than reduced by the advancement of knowledge.

SCIENTIFIC RESEARCH is an entry into
the endless, not a blind alley; solving one
problem, a greater one enters our sight. One
answer breeds a multitude of new questions;
explanations are merely indications of
greater puzzles . . . What appears to be
a center is but a point on the periphery
of another center. The totality of a thing
is actual infinity . . . There is no true
thinker who does not possess an awareness
that his thought is a part of an endless
context, that his ideas are not taken from
air.

SCIENCE is based upon the assumption that there are intelligible laws in nature which can be observed, conceived, and described by the human mind. The scientist did not invent these intricate laws; they were there long before he set about to explore them.

IN WHATEVER WAY, then, we try to conceive the reality of nature—as a mechanism or as an organic order—it is given to us as a meaningful whole, the processes of which are ruled by strict principles. These principles are not only inherent in the actual relations between the components of reality, they are also intrinsically rational if our minds are capable of grasping them. But if rationality is at work in nature, there is no way to account for it without reference to the activity of a supreme intelligence.

Celebration

To CELEBRATE is to contemplate the singularity of the moment and to enhance the singularity of the self. What was shall not be again.

THE BIBLICAL WORDS about the genesis of heaven and earth are not words of information but words of appreciation. The story of creation is not a description of how the world came into being but a song about the glory of the world's having come into being. "And God saw that it was good" (Genesis 1:25). This is the challenge: to reconcile God's view with our experience.

THE DEMAND, as understood in Biblical religion, is to be alert and open to what is happening. What is, happens, comes about. Every moment is a new arrival, a new bestowal. How to welcome the moment? How to respond to the marvel? The cardinal sin is in our failure not to sense the grandeur of the moment, the marvel and mystery of being, the possibility of quiet exaltation.

THE MAN OF OUR TIME is losing the power of celebration. Instead of celebrating, he seeks to be amused or entertained. Celebration is an active state, an act of expressing reverence or appreciation. To be entertained is a passive state—it is to receive pleasure afforded by an amusing act or a spectacle . . . Celebration is a confrontation, giving attention to the transcendent meaning of one's actions.

CELEBRATION is an act of expressing respect or reverence for that which one needs or honors. In modern usage, the term suggests demonstrations, often public demonstrations, of joy and festivity, such as singing, shouting, speechmaking, feasting, and the like. Yet what I mean is not outward ceremony and public demonstration but rather inward appreciation, lending spiritual form to everyday acts.

To CELEBRATE is to share in a greater joy, to participate in an eternal drama. In acts of consumption the intention is to please our own selves; in acts of celebration the intention is to extol God, the spirit, the source of blessing.

WHAT IS THE PURPOSE of knowledge?
We are conditioned to believe that the
purpose of knowledge is to utilize the world.
We forget that the purpose of knowledge
is also to celebrate God. God is both present
and absent. To celebrate is to invoke His
presence concealed in His absence.

THE MIND is in search of rational coherence, the soul in quest of celebration. Knowledge is celebration. Truth is more than equation of thing and thought. Truth transcends and unites both thing and thought. Truth is transcendence.

WE ARE LOSING the power of appreciation; we are losing the ability to sing.
Celebration without appreciation is an
artificial, impersonal ceremony. A renewal
of our strength will depend on our ability
to reopen forgotten resources.

THE MEANING of existence is experienced in moments of exaltation. Man must strive for the summit in order to survive on the ground. His norms must be higher than his behavior, his ends must surpass his needs. The security of existence lies in the exaltation of existence.

THIS IS ONE of the rewards of being human: quiet exaltation, capability for celebration. It is expressed in a phrase which Rabbi Akiba offered to his disciples:

A song every day,
A song every day.

The Religious

Task

————————

THERE ARE no easy solutions for
problems that are at the same time
intensely personal and universal, urgent
and eternal. Technological progress creates
more problems than it solves. Efficiency
experts or social engineering will not redeem
humanity. Important as their contributions
may be, they do not reach the heart of the
problem. Religion, therefore, with its
demands and visions, is not a luxury but
a matter of life and death.

THE MESSAGE of religion is often diluted and distorted by pedantry, externalization, ceremonialism, and superstition. But this precisely is our task: to recall the urgencies, the perpetual emergencies of human existence, the rare cravings of the spirit, the eternal voice of God, to which the demands of religion are the answer.

OUR HEARTS do not breed the desire
to be righteous or holy. While the mind is
endowed with a capacity to grasp higher
ends and to direct our attention to them,
regardless of any material advantage, the
will is naturally inclined to submit to selfish
ends, regardless of the mind's insights.
There is nothing which is less reliable than
man's power for self-denial.

THE MIND is never immune to the
subtle persuasions of the vested interests of
the self. The ultimate goals remain,
therefore, either unapprehended or unvoiced
by the mind. It is religion that must
articulate the unvoiced.

RELIGION BEGINS with the certainty

that something is asked of us, that there

are ends which are in need of us. Unlike

all other values, moral and religious ends

evoke in us a sense of obligation. They

present themselves as tasks rather than as

objects of perception. Thus, religious living

consists in serving ends which are in need

of us.

RELIGION as an institution, the Temple
as an ultimate end, or, in other words,
religion for religion's sake, is idolatry.
The fact is that evil is integral to religion,
not only to secularism. Parochial saint-
liness may be an evasion of duty, an
accommodation to selfishness.

What Is Judaism?

———

THERE IS ONLY one way to define
Jewish religion. It is the awareness of God's
interest in man, the awareness of a covenant,
of a responsibility that lies on Him as well
as on us . . . God is in need of man for
the attainment of His ends, and religion,
as Jewish tradition understands it, is a
way of serving these ends, of which we are
in need, even though we may not be aware
of them; ends which we must learn to feel
the need of.

LIFE IS a partnership of God and man
. . . Authentic vital needs of man's body
and soul are a divine concern. This is why
human life is holy. God is a partner and
partisan in man's struggle for justice, peace,
and holiness, and it is because of His being
in need of man that He entered a covenant
with him for all time, a mutual bond
embracing God and man, a relationship
to which God, not only man, is committed.

THE ESSENCE of Judaism is the awareness of the reciprocity of God and man,
of man's togetherness with Him . . . For
the task of living is His and ours, and so is
the responsibility. We have rights, not
only obligations; our ultimate commitment
is our ultimate privilege.

GOD STANDS in a passionate relationship
to man. His love or anger, His mercy or
disappointment, is an expression of His
profound participation in the history of
Israel and of all men.

THE BIBLE is not a history of the Jewish
people but the story of God's quest for
the righteous man. Because of the failure
of the human species as a whole to
follow in the path of righteousness, it is
an individual: Noah, Abraham—a people:
Israel—or a remnant of the people, on
which the task is bestowed to satisfy that
quest by making every man a righteous man.

WHILE SHUNNING the idea of considering God a means for attaining personal ends, Judaism insists that there is a partnership of God and man, that human needs are God's concern, and that divine ends ought to become human needs . . . Judaism demands the full participation of the person in the service of the Lord.

A MORAL PERSON is a partisan who loves
the love of good. It is not true that love
and obedience cannot live together, that
the good never springs from the heart. To
be free of selfish interests does not mean
to be neutral, indifferent, or devoid of
interests, but, on the contrary, to be a
partisan of the self-surpassing. God does
not dwell beyond the sky. He dwells, we
believe, in every heart that is willing to let
Him in.

THERE IS a breath of God in every man,
a force lying deeper than the stratum of
will, which may be stirred to become an
aspiration strong enough to give direction
and even to run counter to all winds.

THE IDEA of a chosen people does not suggest the preference for a people based upon discrimination among a number of peoples. We do not say that we are a superior people. The "chosen people" means a people approached and chosen by God . . . It signifies not a quality inherent in the people but a relationship between the people and God . . . Judaism is *God's quest for man.* The Bible is a record of God's approach to His people.

WHAT WE HAVE LEARNED from Jewish history is that if a man is not more than human then he is less than human. Judaism is an attempt to prove that in order to be a man you have to be more than a man, that in order to be a people we have to be more than a people. Israel was made to be a "holy people." This is the essence of its dignity and the essence of its merit. Judaism is a link to eternity, kinship with ultimate reality.

Spirit and Flesh

ALLEGIANCE TO Judaism does not imply
defiance of legitimate needs, a tyranny of
the spirit. Prosperity is a worthy goal of
aspiration and a promised reward for good
living. Although there is no celebration
of our animal nature, recognition of its
right and role is never missing. There is an
earnest care for its welfare, needs, and
limitations.

JUDAISM does not despise the carnal. It does not urge us to desert the flesh but to control and to counsel it; to please the natural needs of the flesh so that the spirit should not be molested by unnatural frustrations . . . Judaism teaches us how even the gratification of animal needs can be an act of sanctification.

WE ARE NOT COMMANDED to be
pyromaniacs of the soul. On the contrary,
a need that serves the enhancement of life,
without causing injury to anyone else, is
the work of the Creator, and the wanton
or ignorant destruction or defacement of
His creation is vandalism. "It is indeed
God's gift to man, that he should eat and
drink and be happy as he toils" (Ecclesiastes
3:13).

GOOD LIVING obviously implies control and the relative conquest of passions, but not the renunciation of all satisfaction. Decisive is not the act of conquest but how the victory is utilized. Our ideal is not ruthless conquest but careful alteration of needs. Passion is a many-headed monster, and the goal is achieved through painstaking metamorphosis, rather than by amputation or mutilation.

JUDAISM is not committed to a doctrine
of original sin and knows nothing of the
inherent depravity of human nature.
The word "flesh" did not assume in its
vocabulary the odor of sinfulness; carnal
needs were not thought of as being rooted
in evil. Nowhere in the Bible is found any
indication of the idea that the soul is
imprisoned in a corrupt body, that to seek
satisfaction in this world means to lose
one's soul or to forfeit the covenant with
God, that allegiance to God demands
renunciation of worldly goods.

OUR FLESH is not evil but material for applying the spirit. The carnal is something to be surpassed rather than annihilated. Heaven and earth are equally His creation. Nothing in creation may be discarded or abused. The enemy is not in the flesh; it is in the heart, in the ego.

MAN IS ENDOWED with the ability of being superior to his own self. He does not have to feel helpless in the face of the "evil inclination." He is capable of conquering evil; "God made man upright." If you ask: "Why did He create the 'evil inclination'?," says the Lord: "You turn it evil" (Tanhuma, Bereshit No. 7).

THE ROAD to the sacred leads through the secular. The spiritual rests upon the carnal, like "the spirit that hovers over the face of the water." Jewish living means living according to a system of checks and balances.

HOLINESS does not signify an air
that prevails in the solemn atmosphere
of a sanctuary, a quality reserved for
supreme acts, an adverb of the spiritual,
the distinction of hermits and priests . . .
The strength of holiness lies underground,
in the somatic. It is primarily in the way
in which we gratify physical needs that the
seed of holiness is planted.

ORIGINALLY the holy (*kadosh*) meant that which is set apart, isolated, segregated. In Jewish piety it assumed a new meaning, denoting a quality that is involved, immersed in common and earthly endeavors; carried primarily by individual, private, simple deeds rather than by public ceremonies.

Ennobling the
Common

JUDAISM IS a theology of the common deed, of the trivialities of life, dealing not so much with training for the exceptional as with management of the trivial. The predominant feature in the Jewish pattern of life is unassuming, inconspicuous piety rather than extravagance, mortification, asceticism. Thus, the purpose seems to be to ennoble the common.

PIETY DOES NOT consist in isolated acts,

in sporadic, ephemeral experiences . . .

It is something unremitting, persistent,

unchanging in the soul, a perpetual inner

attitude of the whole man. Like a breeze

in the atmosphere, it runs through all the

deeds, utterances, and thoughts; it is a tenor

of life betraying itself in each trait of

character, each mode of action.

To THE PIOUS MAN, as to the wise one,
mastery over self is a necessity of life. Unlike
the wise man, however, the pious man
feels that he himself is not the autonomous
master but is rather a mediator who
administers his life in the name of God.

THE MOST MAGNIFICENT edifices, most
beautiful temples and monuments of
worldly glory, are repulsive to the man
of piety when they are built by the sweat
and tears of suffering slaves, or erected
through injustice and fraud. Hypocrisy and
pretense of devoutness are more distasteful
to him than open iniquity. But in the
roughened, soiled hands of devoted parents,
or in the maimed bodies and bruised faces
of those who have been persecuted but
have kept faith with God, he may detect
the last great light on earth.

THE PIOUS MAN is ever alert to see behind the appearance of things a trace of the divine, and thus his attitude toward life is one of expectant reverence. Because of this attitude the pious man is at peace with life, in spite of its conflicts. He patiently acquiesces in life's vicissitudes, because he glimpses spiritually their potential meaning. Every experience opens the door into a temple of new light, although the vestibule may be dark and dismal.

THE PIOUS MAN accepts life's ordeals
and its need of anguish, because he
recognizes these as belonging to the totality
of life . . . He is keenly sensitive to pain
and suffering, to adversity and evil in his
own life and in that of others; but he has
the inner strength to rise above grief.

THE PIOUS MAN does not take life for
granted. The weighty business of living
does not cloud for him the miracle of life
and the consciousness that he lives through
God. No routine of social or economic
life dulls his mindfulness of this, the
ineffably wonderful in nature and history.

PIETY cannot consist of specific acts only, such as prayer or ritual observances, but is bound up with all actions, concomitant with all doings, accompanying and shaping all life's business. Man's responsibility to God is the scaffold on which he stands as daily he goes on building life. His every deed, every incident of mind, takes place on this scaffold, so that unremittingly man is at work either building up or tearing down his life, his home, his hope of God.

The Uphill

Struggle

To *pray is to take notice of the wonder, to regain a sense of the mystery that animates all beings, the divine margin in all attainments.* Prayer is *our* humble *answer* to the inconceivable surprise of living. It is all we can offer in return for the mystery by which we live.

To ESCAPE from the mean and
penurious, from calculating and scheming,
is at times the parching desire of man
. . . Prayer clarifies our hope and intentions.
It helps us discover our true aspirations,
the pangs we ignore, the longings we forget.
It is an act of self-purification . . . It
teaches us what to aspire to, implants in
us the ideals we ought to cherish.

PRAYER IS an invitation to God to
intervene in our lives, to let His will
prevail in our affairs; it is the opening of
a window to Him in our will, an effort to
make Him the Lord of our soul. We submit
our interests to His concern, and seek
to be allied with what is ultimately right.

IN A SENSE, prayer begins where
expression ends . . . The soul can only
intimate its persistent striving, the riddle
of its unhappiness, the strain of living
'twixt hope and fear. Where is the tree
that can utter fully the silent passion of
the soil? Words can only open the door,
and we can only weep on the threshold
of our incommunicable thirst after the
incomprehensible.

THE TRUE SOURCE of prayer is not an
emotion but an insight. It is the insight
into the mystery of reality, the *sense of
the ineffable*, that enables us to pray . . .
It is in moments of our being faced with
the mystery of living and dying, of knowing
and not knowing, of love and the inability
of love—that we pray, that *we address
ourselves to Him who is beyond the mystery.*

PRAYER IS NOT a stratagem for occasional use, a refuge to resort to now and then. It is rather like an established residence for the innermost self. All things have a home: the bird has a nest, the fox has a hole, the bee has a hive. A soul without prayer is a soul without a home.

PRAYER IS a perspective from which to behold, from which to respond to, the challenges we face. Man in prayer does not seek to impose his will upon God; he seeks to impose God's will and mercy upon himself. Prayer is necessary to make us aware of our failures, backsliding, transgressions, sins.

GOD IS BEYOND the reach of finite
notions, diametrically opposed to our power
of comprehension. In theory He seems
to be neither here nor now. He is so far
away, an outcast, a refugee in His own
world. It is as if all doors were closed to
Him. To pray is to open a door where both
God and soul may enter. Prayer is arrival,
for Him and for us. To pray is to overcome
distance, to shatter screens, to render
obliquities straight, to heal the break
between God and the world.

A CANDLE of the Lord is the soul of
man, but the soul can become a holocaust,
a fury, a rage. The only cure is to discover
that, over and above the anonymous
stillness in the world, there is a Name
and a waiting. Many young people suffer
from a fear of the self. They do not feel at
home in their own selves. The inner life
is a place of dereliction, a no-man's-land,
inconsolate, weird. The self has become a
place from which to flee. The use of narcotic
drugs is a search for a home.

THE HOUR calls for a revision of
fundamental religious concerns. The wall
of separation between the sacred and the
secular has become a wall of separation
between the conscience and God. In the
Pentateuch, the relation of man to
things of space, to money, to property,
is a fundamental religious problem. In
the affluent society, sins committed with
money may be as grievous as sins committed
with our tongue. We will give account
for what we have done, for what we have
failed to do.

RELIGION as an establishment must
remain separated from the government.
Yet prayer as a voice of mercy, as a cry for
justice, as a plea for gentleness, must not
be kept apart. Let the spirit of prayer
dominate the world. Let the spirit of prayer
interfere in the affairs of man. Prayer is
private, a service of the heart; but let
concern and compassion, born out of
prayer, dominate public life.

WE DO NOT KNOW what to pray for. Should we not pray for the ability to be shocked at atrocities committed by man, for the capacity to be dismayed at our inability to be dismayed? Prayer should be an act of catharsis or purgation of emotions, as well as a process of self-clarification, of examining priorities, of elucidating responsibility.

PRAYER IS meaningless unless it is subversive, unless it seeks to overthrow and to ruin the pyramids of callousness, hatred, opportunism, falsehood. The liturgical movement must become a revolutionary movement, seeking to overthrow the forces that continue to destroy the promise, the hope, the vision.

THE WORLD is aflame with evil and atrocity; the scandal of perpetual desecration of the world cries to high heaven. And we, coming face to face with it, are either involved as callous participants or, at best, remain indifferent onlookers . . . We pray because the disproportion of human misery and human compassion is so enormous. We pray because our grasp of the depth of suffering is comparable to the scope of perception of a butterfly flying over the Grand Canyon. We pray because of the experience of the dreadful incompatibility of how we live and what we sense.

PRAYER requires education, training, reflection, contemplation. It is not enough to join others; it is necessary to build a sanctuary within, brick by brick, instants of meditation, moments of devotion. This is particularly true in an age when overwhelming forces seem to conspire at destroying our ability to pray.

JUST TO BE is a blessing. Just to live is holy. And yet being alive is no answer to the problems of living. To be or not to be is *not* the question. The vital question is: how to be and how not to be. The tendency to forget this vital question is the tragic disease of contemporary man, a disease that may prove fatal, that may end in disaster. To pray is to recollect *passionately* the perpetual urgency of this vital question.

THIS IS the predicament of man. All souls descend a ladder from heaven to this world. Then the ladders are taken away. Once they are in this world, they are called upon from heaven to rise, to come back . . . Each soul seeks the ladder in order to ascend above; but the ladder cannot be found. Most people make no effort to ascend, claiming, How can one rise to heaven without a ladder? However, there are souls which resolve to leap upward, without a ladder. So they jump and fall down. They jump and fall down, until they stop.

RELIGIOUS EXISTENCE is living in
solidarity with God. Yet to maintain such
solidarity involves knowing how to rise,
how to cross an abyss. Vested interests
are more numerous than locusts, and of
solidarity of character there is only a
smattering. Too much devotion is really
too little. It is grave self-deception to assume
that our destiny is just to be human. In
order to be human, one must be more than
human. A person must never stand still.
He must always rise, he must always climb.

WELL-TRODDEN ways lead into swamps. There are no easy ways, there are no simple solutions. What comes easy is not worth a straw. It is a tragic error to assume that the world is flat, that our direction is horizontal. The way is always vertical. It is either up or down; we either climb or fall. Religious existence means struggle uphill.

Why Ritual?

———

WORSHIP IS NOT one thing and living another. Does Judaism consist of sporadic landmarks in the realm of living, of temples in splendid isolation, of festive celebrations on extraordinary days? The synagogue is not a retreat, and that which is decisive is not the performance of rituals at distinguished occasions but how they affect the climate of the entire life.

THE HIGHEST PEAK of spiritual living
is not necessarily reached in rare moments
of ecstasy; the highest peak lies wherever
we are and may be ascended in a common
deed. There can be as sublime a holiness
in fulfilling friendship, in observing dietary
laws, day by day, as in uttering a prayer on
the Day of Atonement.

JEWISH TRADITION maintains that there is no exterritoriality in the realm of the spirit. Economics, politics, dietetics are just as much as ethics within its sphere. It is in man's intimate rather than public life, in the way he fulfills his physiological functions, that character is formed.

JUDAISM BEGINS at the bottom, taking very seriously the forms of one's behavior in relation to the external, even conventional, functions and amenities of life, teaching us how to eat, how to rest, how to act . . . While not prescribing a diet —vegetarian or otherwise—or demanding abstinence from narcotics or stimulants, Judaism is very much concerned with what and how a person ought to eat. A sacred discipline for the body is as important as bodily strength.

"Customs and ceremonies" are an
external affair, an aesthetic delight;
something cherished in academic fraternities
or at graduation exercises at universities.
But since when has aesthetics become
the supreme authority in matters of religion?
Customs, ceremonies are fine, enchanting,
playful. But is Judaism a religion of play?
. . . Let us beware lest we reduce the
Bible to literature, Jewish observance to
good manners, the Talmud to Emily Post.

THERE ARE spiritual reasons which
compel me to feel alarmed when hearing
the terms "customs" and "ceremonies."
What is the worth of celebrating the Seder
on Passover Eve if it is nothing but a
ceremony? An annual re-enactment of
quaint antiquities? Ceremonies end in
boredom, and boredom is the great enemy
of the spirit. A religious act is something
in which the soul must be able to participate;
out of which inner devotion, *kavanah*, must
evolve. But what *kavanah* should I entertain
if entering the *sukkah* is a mere ceremony?

JUDAISM does not stand on ceremonies
. . . Jewish piety is an answer to God,
expressed in the language of *mitzvoth* rather
than in the language of ceremonies and
symbols. The *mitzvah* (religious act) rather
than the ceremony is our fundamental
category.

CEREMONIES, whether in the form of things or in the form of actions, are required by custom and convention; *mitzvoth* are required by Torah. Ceremonies are relevant to man; *mitzvoth* are relevant to God. Ceremonies are folkways; *mitzvoth* are ways to God . . . Ceremonies are created for the purpose of *signifying*; *mitzvoth* were given for the purpose of *sanctifying*. This is their function: to refine, to ennoble, to sanctify man. They confer holiness upon us, whether or not we know exactly what they signify.

THE PRIMARY FUNCTION of the *mitzvoth* is to express *what God wills* . . . a *mitzvah* is a task . . . an act that *ought to be* done . . . Jewish tradition insists that no performance is complete without the participation of the heart. It asks for *kavanah*, for inner participation, not only for external action. *Kavanah* is awareness of the will of God.

Is God Visible?

———

THE SECOND COMMANDMENT implies
more than the prohibition of images; it
implies rejection of all visible symbols for
God; not only images fashioned by man
but also of "any manner of likeness, of any
thing that is in heaven above, or that is
in the earth beneath, or that is in the water
under the earth."

THE FUNDAMENTAL INSIGHT that God
is not and cannot be localized in a thing was
emphatically expressed at a moment in
which it could have been easily forgotten:
at the inauguration of the Temple in
Jerusalem. At that moment Solomon
exclaimed: "But will God in very truth
dwell on earth? Behold, heaven and the
heaven of heavens cannot contain Thee;
how much less this house that I have
built!" (First Kings 8:27). God manifested
himself in *events* rather than in *things*.

THE SYNAGOGUE is not an abode of the deity but a house of prayer, a gathering place for the people. Entering a synagogue, we encounter no objects designed to impart any particular idea to us. Judaism has rejected the picture as a means of representing ideas; it is opposed to pictographic symbols. The only indispensable object is a Scroll to be read, not to be gazed at.

THERE IS no inherent sanctity in Jewish
ritual objects . . . The purpose of ritual
art objects in Judaism is not to inspire love
of God but to enhance our love of doing
a *mitzvah*; to add pleasure to obedience,
delight to fulfillment. Thus, the purpose
is achieved not in direct contemplation but
in combining it with a ritual act; the art
objects have a religious function but no
religious substance.

AND YET there is something in the
world that the Bible does regard as a symbol
of God. It is not a temple or a tree, it is
not a statue or a star. The symbol of God
is *man, every man.* God created man in
His image, in His likeness.

HUMAN LIFE is holy, holier even than the Scrolls of the Torah . . . Reverence for God is shown in our reverence for man. The fear you must feel of offending or hurting a human being must be as ultimate as your fear of God. An act of violence is an act of desecration. To be arrogant toward man is to be blasphemous toward God.

Law

WE BELIEVE that the Jew is committed
to a divine law; that the ultimate standards
are beyond man rather than within man.
We believe that there is a law, the essence
of which is derived from prophetic events
and the interpretation of which is in the
hands of the sages. The supreme imperative
is not merely to believe in God but to do
the will of God.

WHAT IS *law?* A way of dealing with
the most difficult of all problems: life. The
law is a problem to him who thinks that
life is a commonplace. *The law is an answer*
to him who knows that *life is a problem.*

IN JUDAISM, allegiance to God involves a commitment to Jewish law, to a discipline, to specific obligations. These terms, against which modern man seems to feel an aversion, are in fact a part of civilized living. Every one of us who acknowledges allegiance to the state of which he is a citizen is committed to its law and accepts the obligations it imposes upon him.

THE OBJECT of the prophets was to guide and to demand, not only to console and to reassure . . . To the Jewish mind, life is a complex of obligations, and the fundamental category of Judaism is a *demand* rather than a *dogma,* a *commitment* rather than a *feeling* . . . Reverence for the authority of the law is an expression of our love for God.

A DEGREE of self-control is the prerequisite for creative living. Does not a work of art represent the triumph of form over inchoate matter? Emotion controlled by an idea? . . . No one is mature unless he has learned to be engaged in pursuits which require discipline and self-control, and human perfectibility is contingent upon the capacity for self-control.

LIFE ARRANGED according to *halacha* (Jewish law) looks like a mosaic of external deeds, and a superficial view may lead one to think that a person is judged exclusively by how many rituals or deeds of kindness he performs, by how strictly he observes the minutiae of the law, rather than by qualities of inwardness and devotion.

Does Judaism glorify outward action, regardless of intention and motive? Is it action it calls for rather than devotion? Is a person to be judged by what he *does* rather than by what he *is?* Is conduct alone important? Have the *mitzvoth* nothing to say to the soul? Has the soul nothing to say through the *mitzvoth?* We are commanded to carry out specific rituals, such as reciting twice a day "Hear O Israel . . ." or setting the *tefillin* on arm and head. Are we merely commanded *to* recite *"Hear* O Israel . . . God is One," and not *to hear?* Is one's setting of the *tefillin* on head and arm merely a matter of external performance?

No RELIGIOUS ACT is properly fulfilled unless it is done with a willing heart and a craving soul. You cannot worship Him with your body if you do not know how to worship Him with your soul. The relationship between deed and inner devotion must be understood in terms of polarity.

OBSERVANCE must not be reduced to external compliance with the law. Agreement of the heart with the spirit, not only with the letter of the law, is itself a requirement of the law. The goal is to live beyond the dictates of the law; to fulfill the eternal suddenly; to create goodness out of nothing, as it were.

THE LAW, stiff with formality, is a
cry for creativity; a call for nobility
concealed in the form of commandments.
It is not designed to be a yoke, a curb,
a strait-jacket for human action. Above
all, the Torah asks for *love: Thou shalt
love thy God: thou shalt love thy neighbor.*
All observance is training in the art of love.

JUDAISM IS NOT another word for legalism . . . The law is the means, not the end; the way, not the goal. One of the goals is "Ye shall be holy." The Torah is guidance to an end through a law. It is both a vision and a law. Man created in the likeness of God is called upon to re-create the world in the likeness of the vision of God.

THE TORAH is more than a system of laws. The Torah comprises both *halacha* (law) and *agada* (meaning). Like body and soul, they are mutually dependent, and each is a dimension of its own.

Halacha deals with the law; *agada* with the meaning of the law. *Halacha* deals with subjects that can be expressed literally; *agada* introduces us to a realm which lies beyond the range of expression. *Halacha* teaches us how to perform common acts; *agada* tells us how to participate in the eternal drama. *Halacha* gives us knowledge; *agada* gives us aspiration. *Halacha* gives us the norms for action; *agada* the vision of the ends of living. *Halacha* prescribes, *agada* suggests; *halacha* decrees, *agada* inspires; *halacha* is definite; *agada* is allusive.

To MAINTAIN that the essence of Judaism consists exclusively of *halacha* is as erroneous as to maintain that the essence of Judaism consists exclusively of *agada*. The interrelationship of *halacha* and *agada* is the very heart of Judaism. *Halacha* without *agada* is dead; *agada* without *halacha* is wild.

THERE IS no *halacha* without *agada*,
and no *agada* without *halacha*. We must
neither disparage the body nor sacrifice
the spirit. The body is the discipline, the
pattern, the law; the spirit is inner devotion,
spontaneity, freedom . . . Our task is to
learn how to maintain a harmony between
the demands of *halacha* and the spirit of
agada.

The Human and

the Holy

———

A *mitzvah* is an act which God and man *have in common*. The oldest form of piety is expressed in the Bible as walking *with God* . . . "It has been told thee, O man, what is good, and what the Lord doth require of thee: only to do justly, to love mercy and to *walk humbly with thy God*" (Micah 6:8).

As SURELY as we are driven to live, we are driven to serve spiritual ends that surpass our own interests. "The good drive" is not invented by society but is something which makes society possible; not an accidental function but of the very essence of man. We may lack a clear perception of its meaning, but we are moved by the horror of its violation . . . *Mitzvoth* are *spiritual ends.*

THE HEART is often a lonely voice in the marketplace of living. Man may entertain lofty ideals and behave like the ass that, as the saying goes, "carries gold and eats thistles." The problem of the soul is how to live nobly in an animal environment; how to persuade and train the tongue and the senses to behave in agreement with the insights of the soul.

IN THIS WORLD, music is played on physical instruments, and to the Jew the *mitzvoth* are the instruments on which the holy is carried out. If man were only mind, worship in thought would be the form in which to commune with God. But man is body and soul, and his goal is so to live that both "his heart and his flesh should sing to the living God."

EVEN BEFORE Israel was told in the
Ten Commandments what to do, it was
told what *to be: a holy people*. To perform
deeds of holiness is to absorb the holiness
of deeds . . . The good deeds are for
the sake of man . . . The goal is not that
a ceremony be *performed*: the goal is that
man be *transformed*; to worship the Holy
in order to be holy. The purpose of the
mitzvoth is to *sanctify* man.

THE NOUN, *"kavanah,"* denotes
meaning, purpose, motive, and intention
. . . the state of being aware of what we
are doing . . . *Kavanah* is the awareness
of God rather than the awareness of
duty. Such awareness is more than an
attitude of the mind; it is an act of valuation
or *appreciation* of being commanded, of
living in a covenant, of the opportunity
to act in agreement with God.

APPRECIATION is not the same as reflection. It is an attitude of the whole person. It is one's being drawn to the preciousness of an object or a situation. To sense the preciousness of being able to listen to an imperative of God, to be perceptive of the unique worth of doing a *mitzvah*, is the beginning of higher *kavanah*.

A *mitzvah* is like a musical score,
and its performance is not a mechanical
accomplishment but an artistic act. The
music in a score is open only to him who
has music in his soul. It is not enough to
play the notes; one must *be* what he *plays*.
It is not enough to do the *mitzvah*; one must
live what he *does*. The goal is to find
access to the sacred deed.

THE JEWISH WAY of living is an answer
to a supreme human problem, namely:
How must man, a being who is in essence
the likeness of God, think, feel, and act?
How can he live in a way compatible with
the presence of God? . . . All *mitzvoth*
are means of evoking in us the awareness
of living in the neighborhood of God, of
living in the holy dimension . . . *Every
act* of man is an encounter of the human
and the holy.

THE MEANING of a *mitzvah* is in
its power of sanctification . . . The soul
is illumined by sacred acts . . . The
purpose of all *mitzvoth* is to refine man.
They were given for the benefit of man:
to protect and to ennoble him, to discipline
and to inspire him. We ennoble the self
by disclosing the divine . . . Our task
is to let the divine emerge from our deeds.

MITZVAH denotes not only commandment but also *the law,* man's *obligation* to fulfill the law, and *the act* of fulfilling the obligation or the deed, particularly an act of benevolence or charity. Its meanings range from the acts performed by the high priest in the temple to the most humble gesture of kindness to one's fellow man.

THE BASIC TERM of Jewish living is
mitzvah rather than *din* (law). The law
serves us as a source of knowledge about
what is and what is not to be regarded as
a *mitzvah*. The act itself, what a person
does with that knowledge, is determined not
only by what the law describes but also by
that which the law cannot enforce: the
freedom of the heart.

Prophet and

Prophecy

THE PROPHET is a man who feels fiercely. God has thrust a burden upon his soul, and he is bowed and stunned at man's fierce greed. Frightful is the agony of man; no human voice can convey its full terror. Prophecy is the voice that God has lent to the silent agony, a voice to the plundered poor, to the profaned riches of the world. It is a form of living, a crossing point of God and man. God is raging in the prophet's words.

CIVILIZATION may come to an end
and the human species disappear. This
world, no mere shadow of ideas in an upper
sphere, is real but not absolute; the world's
reality is contingent upon compatibility
with God. While others are intoxicated with
the here and now, the prophet has a vision
of an end.

To THE PROPHET, no subject is as worthy of consideration as the plight of man. Indeed, God himself is described as reflecting over the plight of man rather than as contemplating eternal ideas . . . In the prophet's message nothing that has bearing upon good and evil is small or trite in the eyes of God.

WE and the prophet have no language
in common. To us the moral state of
society, for all its stains and spots, seems
fair and trim; to the prophet it is dreadful.
So many deeds of charity are done, so
much decency radiates day and night; yet,
to the prophet, satiety of the conscience
is prudery and flight from responsibility.
Our standards are modest; our sense
of injustice tolerable, timid; our moral
indignation impermanent; yet human
violence is interminable, unbearable,
permanent.

THE WORDS of the prophet are stern, sour, stinging. But behind his austerity is love and compassion for mankind . . . Indeed, every prediction of disaster is in itself an exhortation to repentance . . . He begins with *a message of doom*; he concludes with *a message of hope* . . . His essential task is to declare the word of God to the here and now; to disclose the future in order to illuminate what is involved in the present.

ABOVE ALL, the prophets remind us of
the moral state of a people: Few are
guilty, but all are responsible.

THE PROPHET is a lonely man. He alienates the wicked as well as the pious, the cynics as well as the believers, the priests and the princes, the judges and the false prophets. But to be a prophet means to challenge and to defy and to cast out fear.

THE PROPHET is a watchman
(Hosea 9:8), a servant (Amos 3:7;
Jeremiah 25:4; 26:5), a messenger of
God (Haggai 1:13), "an assayer and
tester" of the people's ways (Jeremiah
6:27, RSV) . . . The prophet's eye is
directed to the contemporary scene; society
and its conduct are the main theme of his
speeches. Yet his ear is inclined to God
. . . His true greatness is his ability to
hold God and man in a single thought.

WHEN THE PROPHETS appeared, they
proclaimed that might is not supreme,
that the sword is an abomination, that
violence is obscene. The sword, they said,
shall be destroyed.

> They shall beat their swords into
>   plowshares,
> And their spears into pruning hooks;
> Nation shall not lift up sword against
>   nation,
> Neither shall they learn war any more.
>
> Isaiah 2:4

THE PROPHETS did not isolate the evil
of war, and they seem to have regarded it
as the extension of a condition that prevails
even in time of peace.

Noise, fury, tumult are usually
associated with battles of war, when
nation seeks to destroy nation. The cheating,
the cunning, the humiliations by which
individuals seek to destroy each other are
pursued discreetly, with no one feeling
hurt, consciously, except the victim.

As IT WAS in the age of the prophets,
so it is in nearly every age: we all go mad,
not only individually, but also nationally.
We check manslaughter and isolated
murders; we wage wars and slaughter whole
peoples . . . We measure manhood by
the sword and are convinced that history
is ultimately determined on the fields of
battle.

Righteousness and peace are interdependent (Psalms 85:10). "The effect of righteousness will be peace, And the result of righteousness quietness and trust for ever" (Isaiah 32:17).

THE PROPHET may be regarded as
the first universal man in history; he is
concerned with, and addresses himself to,
all men. It was not an emperor but a prophet
who first conceived of the unity of all men.

OTHERS have considered history from the point of view of power, judging its course in terms of victory and defeat, of wealth and success; the prophets look at history from the point of view of justice, judging its course in terms of righteousness and corruption, of compassion and violence.

THIS IS WHAT the prophets discovered: history is a nightmare. There are more scandals, more acts of corruption, than are dreamed of in philosophy. It would be blasphemous to believe that what we witness is the end of God's creation. It is an act of evil to accept the state of evil as either inevitable or final. The way man acts is a disgrace, and it must not go on forever.

RIGHTEOUSNESS goes beyond justice. Justice is strict and exact, giving each person his due. Righteousness implies benevolence, kindness, generosity . . . Justice may be legal; righteousness is associated with a burning compassion for the oppressed.

THE PHENOMENON of prophecy is predicated upon the assumption that man is both in need of, and entitled to, divine guidance. For God to reveal His word through the prophet to His people is an act of justice or an act of seeking to do justice. The purpose of prophecy is to maintain the covenant, to establish the right relationship between God and man.

IN A SENSE, the calling of the prophet may be described as that of an advocate or champion, speaking for those who are too weak to plead their own cause. Indeed, the major activity of the prophets was *interference*, remonstrating about wrongs inflicted on other people, meddling in affairs which were seemingly neither their concern nor their responsibility.

JUSTICE IS an interpersonal relationship, implying both a claim and a responsibility. Justice bespeaks a situation that transcends the individual, demanding from everyone a certain abnegation of self, defiance of self-interest, disregard of self-respect. The necessity of submitting to a law is derived from the necessity of identifying oneself with what concerns other individuals or the whole community of men.

THE PROPHETS proclaimed that justice
is omnipotent, that right and wrong are
dimensions of world history, not merely
modes of conduct. The existence of the
world is contingent upon right and
wrong . . . The validity of justice and
the motivation for its exercise lie in the
blessings it brings to man . . . Justice
exists in relation to a person . . . An
act of injustice is condemned, not because
the law is broken, but because a person
has been hurt.

The Sabbath

JUDAISM IS A *religion of time* aiming at the *sanctification of time*. Unlike the space-minded man to whom time is unvaried, iterative, homogenous, to whom all hours are alike, qualityless, empty shells, the Bible senses the diversified character of time. There are no two hours alike. Every hour is unique and the only one given at the moment, exclusive and endlessly precious.

JUDAISM TEACHES US to be attached to *holiness in time,* to be attached to sacred events, to learn how to consecrate sanctuaries that emerge from the magnificent stream of a year. The Sabbaths are our great cathedrals; and our Holy of Holies is a shrine that neither the Romans nor the Germans were able to burn; a shrine that even apostasy cannot easily obliterate: the Day of Atonement. According to the ancient rabbis, it is not the observance of the Day of Atonement but the Day itself, the "essence of the Day," which, with man's repentance, atones for the sins of man.

JEWISH RITUAL may be characterized
as the art of significant forms in time,
as *architecture of time*. Most of its
observances—the Sabbath, the New Moon,
the festivals, the Sabbatical and the Jubilee
year—depend on a certain hour of the day
or a season of the year. It is the evening,
morning, or afternoon that brings with it
the call to prayer. The main themes of faith
lie in the realm of time. We remember the
day of the exodus from Egypt, the day
when Israel stood at Sinai; and our Messianic
hope is the expectation of a day, of the end
of days.

THE MEANING of the Sabbath is to celebrate time rather than space. Six days a week we live under the tyranny of things of space; on the Sabbath we try to become attuned to *holiness in time*. It is a day on which we are called upon to share in what is eternal in time, to turn from the results of creation to the mystery of creation; from the world of creation to the creation of the world.

THE SABBATH as a day of rest is not for the purpose of recovering one's lost strength and becoming fit for the forth-coming labor. The Sabbath is a day for the sake of life. Man is not a beast of burden and the Sabbath is not for the purpose of enhancing the efficiency of his work.

CONTINUOUS AUSTERITY may severely dampen, yet levity would certainly obliterate the spirit of the day . . . It must always be remembered that the Sabbath is not an occasion for diversion or frivolity; not a day to shoot fireworks or to turn somersaults, but an opportunity to mend our tattered lives; to collect rather than to dissipate time.

To SANCTIFY the seventh day does not mean: Thou shalt mortify thyself, but, on the contrary: Thou shalt sanctify it with all thy heart, with all thy soul, and with all thy senses. "Sanctify the Sabbath by choice meals, by beautiful garments; delight your soul with pleasure and I will reward you for this very pleasure."

"SIX DAYS shalt thou labor and do all thy work; but the seventh day is Sabbath unto the Lord thy God." Just as we are commanded to keep the Sabbath, we are commanded to labor. "Love work . . ." The duty to work for six days is just as much a part of God's covenant with man as the duty to abstain from work on the seventh day.

THE SEVENTH DAY is the armistice in man's cruel struggle for existence, a truce in all conflicts, personal and social, peace between man and man, man and nature, peace within man; a day on which handling money is considered a desecration, on which man avows his independence of that which is the world's chief idol. The seventh day is the exodus from tension.

IN THE tempestuous ocean of time and
toil there are islands of stillness where
man may enter a harbor and reclaim his
dignity. The island is the seventh day,
the Sabbath, a day of detachment from
things, instruments, and practical affairs,
as well as of attachment to the spirit.

THE SABBATH is a day on which
we are what we are, regardless of whether
we are learned or not, of whether our career
is a success or a failure; it is a day of
independence of social conditions . . . All
week we may ponder and worry whether
we are rich or poor, whether we succeed
or fail in our occupations; whether we
accomplish or fall short of reaching our goals.

THE SABBATH is no time for personal anxiety or care, for any activity that might dampen the spirit of joy. The Sabbath is no time to remember sins, to confess, to repent, or even to pray for relief or anything we might need . . . Fasting, mourning, demonstrations of grief are forbidden. The period of mourning is interrupted by the Sabbath . . . One must abstain from toil and strain on the seventh day, even from the strain in the service of God.

WHEN ALL WORK is brought to a standstill, the candles are lit. Just as creation began with the words "Let there be light!" so does the celebration of creation begin with the kindling of lights. It is the woman who ushers in the joy and sets up the most exquisite symbol, light, to dominate the atmosphere of the home. And the world becomes a place of rest.

One World

IN OUR OWN AGE we have been forced
into the realization that, in terms of human
relations, there will be either one world
or no world. But political and moral unity
as a goal presupposes unity as a source.

ETERNITY IS another word for unity

. . . Unity is a task, not a condition . . .

The universe is in a state of spiritual disorder

. . . The goal of all efforts is to bring

about the restitution of the unity of God

and world.

THE WORLD could not exist at all
except as one; deprived of unity, it would
not be a cosmos but chaos, an agglomeration
of countless possibilities . . . Life is
tangled, fierce, fickle. We cannot remain
in agreement with all goals. We are
constantly compelled to make a choice,
and the choice of one goal means the
forsaking of another.

GOD WILL RETURN to us when we shall be willing to let Him in —into our banks and factories, into our Congress and clubs, into our courts and investigating committees, into our homes and theaters. For God is everywhere or nowhere, the Father of all men or no man, concerned about everything or nothing. Only in His presence shall we learn that the glory of man is not in his will to power but in his power of compassion.

WHEN GOD BECOMES our form of
thinking, we begin to sense all men in one
man, the whole world in a grain of sand,
eternity in a moment. To worldly ethics,
one human being is less than two human
beings; to the religious mind, if a man
has caused a single soul to perish, it is as
though he had caused a whole world to
perish, and if he has saved a single soul,
it is as though he had saved a whole world.*

* Mishnah Sanhedrin, 4, 5.

ACCORDING TO the Kabbalah, redemption is not an event that will take place
all at once at "the end of days" or
something that concerns the Jewish people
alone. It is a continual process, taking place
at every moment. Man's good deeds are
single acts in the long drama of redemption,
and not only the people of Israel but the
whole universe must be redeemed.

THE MEANING of man's life lies in
his perfecting the universe. He has to
distinguish, gather, and redeem the
sparks of holiness scattered throughout
the darkness of the world. This service
is the motive of all precepts and good deeds.

JUDAISM TODAY is the least known religion . . . The tasks, begun by the patriarchs and prophets and continued by their descendants, are now entrusted to us. We are either the last Jews or those who will hand over the entire past to generations to come. We will either forfeit or enrich the legacy of ages.

JUDAISM IS the track of God in the wilderness of oblivion. By being what we are, namely Jews; by attuning our own yearning to the lonely holiness in this world, we will aid humanity more than by any particular service we may render.

THE GREAT DREAM of Judaism is not to raise priests but a people of priests; to consecrate all men, not only some men.

Judaism is *the art of surpassing civilization*, sanctification of time, sanctification of history.

THE TASK of Jewish philosophy today is not only to describe the essence but also to set forth the universal relevance of Judaism, the bearings of its demands upon the chance of man to remain human.

CREATION is not an act that happened once upon a time, once and forever. The act of bringing the world into existence is a continuous process. God called the world into being, and that call goes on. There is this present moment because God is present. Every instant is an act of creation. A moment is not a terminal but a flash, a signal of Beginning. Time is perpetual innovation, a synonym for continuous creation.

WE OFTEN FAIL in trying to understand Him, not because we do not know how to extend our concepts far enough, but because we do not know how to begin close enough. To think of God is not to find Him as an object in our minds but to find ourselves in Him.

RABBI MOSHE of Kobrin once said
to his disciples: "Do you want to know
where God is?" He took a piece of bread
from the table, showed it to everybody,
and said: "Here is God."

The Bible

———

JUDAISM IS a confrontation with the Bible, and a philosophy of Judaism must be a confrontation with the thought of the Bible.

THE BIBLE is an answer to the question: how to sanctify life. And if we say we feel no need for sanctification, we only prove that the Bible is indispensable. Because it is the Bible that teaches us how to feel the need for sanctification.

THE BIBLE showed man his indepen-
dence of nature, his superiority to conditions,
and called on him to realize the tremendous
implications of simple acts. The degree of
our appreciation of the Bible is, therefore,
determined by the degree of our sensitivity
to the divine dignity of human deeds.
The insight into the divine implications of
human life is the distinct message of the
Bible.

HE WHO SEEKS an answer to the most
pressing question, What is living? will find
an answer in the Bible: Man's destiny is
to be a partner rather than a master. There
is a task, a law, and a way: the task is
redemption; the law, to do justice, to love
mercy; and the way is the secret of being
human and holy.

THE BIBLE IS *holiness in words* . . .
It does not deal with divinity but with
humanity . . . Judaism is not a prophetic
religion but a people's religion . . . Biblical
revelation took place not for the benefit
of the prophets but for the sake of Israel
and all men.

IN ALMOST EVERY CULT and religion, certain beings, things, places, or actions are considered to be holy. However, the idea of holiness of an entire people, Israel as a holy people, is without parallel in human history . . . Only extraordinary, super- natural events in the life of all of Israel would have made the usage of the term "a holy people" possible.

To DENY the divine origin of the
Bible is to brand the entire history of
spiritual efforts and attainments in Judaism,
Christianity, and Islam as the outgrowth
of a colossal lie, the triumph of a deception
which captured the finest souls for more
than two thousand years.

THE BIBLE IS the book of God.

Disclosing the love of God for man, it

opens our eyes to see the unity of that which

is meaningful to mankind and that which

is sacred to God, showing us how to make

a nation, not only the life of an individual,

holy.

God and Man

———

Is IT MEANINGFUL to speak of communication between God and man? If a stream of energy that is stored up in the sun and the soil can be channeled into a blade of grass, why should it be excluded that the spirit of God reached into the minds of men? There is such a distance between the sun and a flower. Can a flower, worlds away from the source of energy, attain a perception of its origin?

DID IT EVER HAPPEN that God disclosed His will to some men for the benefit of all men? Can a drop of water ever soar to behold, even for a moment, the stream's distant source? In prophecy it is as if the sun communed with the flower, as if the source sent out a current to reach a drop.

ARE WE, then, because of the indescribability of revelation, justified in rejecting *a priori* as untrue the assertion of the prophets that, at certain hours in Israel's history, the divine came in touch with a few chosen souls? That the creative source of our own selves addressed itself to man?

IF THERE ARE moments in which genius
speaks for all men, why should we deny
that there are moments in which a voice
speaks for God? that the source of goodness
communicates its way to the human mind?

THE LEADING EXPONENTS of Jewish
thought exhort us not to imagine that God
speaks, or that a sound is produced by
Him through organs of speech . . . In
being "told that God addressed the prophets
and spoke to them, our minds are merely
to receive a notion that there is a divine
knowledge to which the prophets attain
. . . We must not suppose that in speaking
God employed voice or sound."

The Living God

THE CENTRAL THOUGHT of Judaism is
the living God . . . The supreme problem
in any philosophy of Judaism is: What
are the grounds for man's believing in the
realness of the living God? Is man at all
capable of discovering such grounds?

To THE GREEKS, who take the world for granted, nature, order, is the answer. To the Biblical mind in its radical amazement, nature, order, is not an answer but a problem: Why is there order, being, at all?

To THE BIBLICAL MAN, the power of God is behind all phenomena, and he is more concerned to know the will of God who governed nature than to know the order of nature itself. Important and impressive as nature is to him, God is vastly more so. That is why Psalm 104 is a hymn to God rather than an ode to the cosmos.

THE BIBLICAL MAN never asks: Is
there a God? The questions advanced in
the Bible are of a different kind.

Lift up your eyes on high
and see, Who created these?
It reflects a situation in which the mind
stands *face to face* with the mystery rather
than with its own concepts.

GOD IS CONCERN, not only power. God is He *to whom we are accountable*. In the wake of religious insight, we retain an awareness that the transcendent God is *He to Whom our conscience is open*.

WHATEVER THE ORIGIN of conscience
may have been, there are few things in
the realm of human life that are of
such fundamental significance . . . Our
conscience, our moral sense claim that
there is a moral relationship between God
and human. What is indubitably certain
is our sense of obligation to answer for
our conduct.

PROPHECY consists in the proclamation
of the divine *pathos*, expressed in the
language of the prophets as love, mercy,
or anger. Behind the various manifestations
of His pathos is one motive, one need: the
divine need for human righteousness.

GOD'S EXISTENCE—what may it mean?

. . . If creation is conceived as a voluntary

activity of the Supreme Being, it implies

a concern with that which is coming into

being. In ascribing a transitive concern

to God, we ascribe to Him not a psychic

but a spiritual characteristic, not an

emotional but a moral attitude . . .

Creation is not an act that happened once

but a continuous process . . . God in the

universe is a spirit of concern for life.

THE CLAIM of the Bible is absurd, unless we are ready to comprehend that the world as scrutinized and depicted by science is but a thin surface of the profoundly unknown. Order is only one of the aspects of nature; its reality is a mystery given but not known.

IT IS the dimension of time wherein man meets God, wherein man becomes aware that every instant is an act of creation, a Beginning, opening up new roads for ultimate realizations. Time is the presence of God in the world of space, and it is within time that we are able to sense the unity of all beings.

MAN LIVES in a spiritual order.
Moments of insight, moments of decision,
moments of prayer, may be insignificant
in the world of space, yet they put life
into focus.

How DO WE KNOW that it is a living
God, the Creator of heaven and earth,
whose concern reached the soul? . . .
Oneness is the norm, the standard, and
the goal . . . Only that which is good for
all men is good for every man.

References

G   *God in Search of Man:* A Philosophy of Judaism. New York: Farrar, Straus and Giroux, 1955; also, Octagon Books, 1972.

M   *Man Is Not Alone:* A Philosophy of Religion. New York: Farrar, Straus and Giroux, 1972; also, Harper & Row, 1951.

Q   *Man's Quest for God.* New York: Charles Scribner Sons, 1954.

W   *Who Is Man?* Stanford, Calif.: Stanford University Press, 1965.

F   *The Insecurity of Freedom:* Essays on Human Existence. New York: Farrar, Straus and Giroux, 1966.

E   *The Earth Is the Lord's.* New York: Harper & Row, 1969.

S   *The Sabbath.* New York: Farrar, Straus and Giroux, 1951; also, Harper & Row, 1957.

P   *The Prophets.* New York: Harper & Row, 1962.

JH   *Jewish Heritage,* vol. 14, no. 2. Summer, 1972.

CJ   "On Prayer." *Conservative Judaism,* vol. xxv, no. 1, 1970.